a pocketful of
RHYME
Imagination for a new generation

2006 Poetry Competition for 7-11 year-olds

YoungWriters

Lincolnshire
Edited by Angela Fairbrace

 Young**Writers**

First published in Great Britain in 2007 by:
Young Writers
Remus House
Coltsfoot Drive
Peterborough
PE2 9JX
Telephone: 01733 890066
Website: www.youngwriters.co.uk

SB ISBN 1 84602 741 1

Foreword

Young Writers was established in 1991 and has been passionately devoted to the promotion of reading and writing in children and young adults ever since. The quest continues today. Young Writers remains as committed to the nurturing of poetic and literary talent as ever.

This year's Young Writers competition has proven as vibrant and dynamic as ever and we are delighted to present a showcase of the best poetry from across the UK and in some cases overseas. Each poem has been selected from a wealth of *A Pocketful Of Rhyme* entries before ultimately being published in this, our fourteenth primary school poetry series.

Once again, we have been supremely impressed by the overall quality of the entries we have received. The imagination, energy and creativity which has gone into each young writer's entry made choosing the poems a challenging and often difficult but ultimately hugely rewarding task - the general high standard of the work submitted ensured this opportunity to bring their poetry to a larger appreciative audience.

We sincerely hope you are pleased with this final collection and that you will enjoy *A Pocketful Of Rhyme Lincolnshire* for many years to come.

Contents

Philip Lawson (9)   37
Mae Davies (10)   38

Killingholme Primary School
Sophie Smylie (10)   39
Hayden Taylor (9)   40
Oliver Bates (10)   41
Nathan Oxley (10)   42
Jack Coupland (9)   43
Leah Kirkby (10)   44
James Stockdale (9)   45
Victoria Vessey (10)   46
Amy Price (8)   47
Sophie Stuart (10)   48

Humberston CE Primary School
Georgia Copley (9)   49
Francesca Wood (9)   50
Joshua Hargreaves (9)   51
Oliver Furneaux (9)   52
Mia-Fay Harper (9)   53
Oliver Seddon (9)   54
Lucy Catlyn (9)   55
Joshua Blissett (9)   56
Trumann Capes (9)   57
Amber Bacon (9)   58
Joseph Baker (9)   59
Jack Ranson (9)   60
Liam Pettinger (9)   61
Sam Lord (9)   62
Niamh Tuplin (9)   63
Emily Cook (9)   64
Emily Stevenson (9)   65
Brad Gooseman (9)   66
Charlie-Jade Cowling (9)   67
Henry Tasker (9)   68
Mollie Horton (9)   69
Joe O'Hagan (9)   70
Jordan Graves (9)   71
Joshua Winchester (10)   72
Louis Townell (10)   73

Emma Brown (9)   74
Ella Goldsmith (10)   75
Sophie Goldsmith (10)   76
Jake Curtis (10)   77
Daniel Pattison (10)   78
Layla Albery (9)   79
Alisha Woulfe-Flanagan (9)   80
Sophie Pattison (8)   81
Jack Tutass (7)   82
Rosie Pettinger (7)   83
Rawan Jaibaji (8)   84
Katherine Brown (8)   85
Lani Frith (8)   86
Lewis Atkin (8)   87
Dylan Thomas (8)   88
Dilasha Gurung (8)   89
Alex Booker (9)   90
Charlie Spencer (8)   91
Alexandra Badger-Young (9)   92
Abigail James (8)   93
Harry Pask (8)   94
Jacob Boden (9)   95
Eden Gabbitas (8)   96
Alexander Masterton (9)   97
Daniella Baker (8)   98
Ella Fearn (9)   99
Charlie Goodhand (9)   100
Patrick Curtis (8)   101
Chloe Fletcher (8)   102
Sam Hotson (9)   103
Danielle Gorrod (10)   104
Jessica Cubbison (10)   105
Georgia Strong (10)   106
Olivia Strong (10)   107
Connor Masterton (10)   108
Mark Siddle (10)   109
Bradley Sadler (10)   110
Ashley Fletcher (10)   111
Daisy Seddon (10)   112
Lyndsey Loveday (10)   113
Saskia Wilbourne-Davy (10)   114

Lisle Marsden CE Primary School

Jackson Woods (7)	115
Joshua Parrish (7)	116
Lauren Stafford (7)	117
Olivia Probert (7)	118
Kayleigh Wild (7)	119
Ben Fuller (7)	120
David Radford (7)	121
William Seed (8)	122
Lou Trigg (7)	123
Alex Dunham (7)	124
Megan Hawes (7)	125
Kerryn Shortland (8)	126
Natasha Ahmed (7)	127
Bradley Kirk (7)	128
Joseph Short (7)	129
Luke Codd (8)	130
Liam Murtagh (7)	131
Loretta Hall (8)	132
Oliver Baxter (8)	133
Jack Crichton (8)	134
Zara Dawson (8)	135
Louis Wheelton (8)	136
Thomas Chessman (8)	137
Rebecca Burrows (8)	138
Jacque Barnes (8)	139
Alfie Ney (7)	140
Tyler Wells (8)	141
Jack Paddison (8)	142
William Paddison (7)	143
Connor Neal (8)	144
Jaelle Walker (8)	145

Market Rasen CE Primary School

Nicholas Hawke (10)	146
Rebecca Dame (9)	147
Frances Haley (9)	148
George Bennett (9)	149
Amber Bowyer (9)	150
Mason Dawson (9)	151
Kate Cooling (9)	152

Harry Weatherall (9)	153
Georgia Eshelby (9)	154
Megan Gardner (7)	155
Esther Robinson (7)	156
Holly Butterworth (7)	157
Daniel Young (9)	158
Aaron Briggs (10)	159
Emma-Jane Hordon (9)	160
Riegan Carlton (7)	161
Alice Rice (10)	162
Kieron Paul (7)	163
Jarrad Dawson (7)	164
Abbie Sellars (8)	165
Oliver Boylan (7)	166
Alexander Hodgkinson (7)	167

Pinchbeck East Primary School

Laura Walott (7)	168
Lucy Seymour (8)	169
Megan Edwards (8)	170
Amy Wilson (8)	171
Layla Alexander (8)	172

Winterton Junior School

Lucy Barley (9)	173
Corrianne Gray (8)	174
Danielle Preskey (8)	175
Holly Welsh (9)	176
Molly Brocklebank (8)	177
Georgia Ashton (9)	178
Sophie Thompson (9)	179
Benjamin Johns (8)	180
Julian Buckley (8)	181
Kirsty Nundy (9)	182
Natalia Dobbs (7)	183
Jessica Ashton (10)	184
Emma Reid (7)	185
Jessica Barley (8)	186
Katie Waters (7)	187
Chloe Darnill (8)	188
Alysha Harvey (7)	189

The Poems

A Star

You're a firework, exploding in the cold, dark air, or
100 million light bulbs, lighting up a winter's moon.

You're golden night-time torches, lighting up a person's path,
Helping them on their way.

You're a beautiful, glimmering diamond, waiting to be found,
In an oak treasure chest.

You're a marble, so bright, you could light up a galaxy.

You're a star!

Matthew Yeadon (9)
Burgh-Le-Marsh CE Primary School

Night

Night vanishes in daytime hours
She comes in and grabs the light by the collar
And chucks him out.
She is the daytime's worst enemy.
Night lurks around every corner.
Light is afraid of night because night chucks light out,
And starts a fight.
Dark heart like a black hole, vanishes light at night-time hours.

Luke Sheppard (10)
Burgh-Le-Marsh CE Primary School

Night

Slowly the sky curtains close
And night lurks over us.
We should look out
For she could just pounce.

She wears a black cloak
Printed with stars,
She throws small objects
That turn out shooting stars.

James Wilson (11)
Burgh-Le-Marsh CE Primary School

Night

Night is a young female,
Night lives in a dark, shadowy, gloomy cave,
She wears a long, dark, hooded cape,
With a long, endless ultramarine gown.
Her eyes twinkle like stars in the midnight sky,
She slinks about the sky casting darkness,
She also dislikes her sister Sunrise.

Hollie Baxter (10)
Burgh-Le-Marsh CE Primary School

Star

Diamonds
Of gold
Dancing into
The night sky.
Petals scattered all
Over at dusk.
Exploded sparkles of fire.
The best dancing diamonds are the
Sun of the sky.
The glowing of the moon's
Rays.
Stars begging to leave the dance floor
The sun makes them sleep
And wait till I play
Again.

Elizabeth Ransom (9)
Burgh-Le-Marsh CE Primary School

Pipi, My Sister

She is a sun setting on the beach.
She is melted chocolate on my hand.
She makes me laugh when I am sad.
She is water going down a river.

Edward Walker (9)
Burgh-Le-Marsh CE Primary School

Mum

You're the pink rose cheeks glowing in the daylight.
You're the pizza cooking in the oven.
You're the happiness inside me.
You're the water dripping down my throat.
You're the roof of the Wendy house.
You're the ¾ lengths I wear.
You're the pop music I listen to.
You're the mum I love.

Olivia Green (9)
Burgh-Le-Marsh CE Primary School

My Family

You are the waters of Scotland trickling down rocks.
The mooing cows on the glowing fields.
Chocolate melting succulently in my mouth.

You are the music running through my head every day.
The Arctic Monkeys and The Kooks keeping me singing.
You are the hot burning tea, trickling down my throat.

Samantha Geaghan (9)
Burgh-Le-Marsh CE Primary School

Star Poem

Your
Points
Play the
Piano all
Night long.
A bright light lighting up the darkness.
You glitter and shine on the world.
You're a beautiful daisy bursting with music.
A fiery ball glittering and
Shimmering bright in the
Twilight sky.

Eliza Clark (9)
Burgh-Le-Marsh CE Primary School

Mum

You're a beautiful purple sunset,
You're home-made pasta in the warm oven,
You're a lovely purple, soft blanket.

You're the delicious juice running down my throat,
You're the wonderful happiness inside me,
You're the juice inside my happiness.

Yasmin Broughton (9)
Burgh-Le-Marsh CE Primary School

Star

Star you are a champion,
A champ in other words,
You are in first place,
With a medal around your neck,
You are a runner bean that's
Running faster than light,
You are a jumping bean,
Jumping in the night.

Callum Grebby (9)
Burgh-Le-Marsh CE Primary School

My Brother

You're
A daisy
In the moonlight
Shining
So bright
You're a moon
Growing through frozen rings.
You're a cake, a golden cake with a golden flower.
You're a fiery sunflower
Opening in daylight.

Kieran Cardwell (9)
Burgh-Le-Marsh CE Primary School

Star

While the star
Twinkles, music
Flows through my mind,
Booming on its piano.
While the saxophone plays
He plays his music that irritates my head,
His golden shine, lights up the night,
Why, oh star, do you shine so bright?

Daniel Scott (9)
Burgh-Le-Marsh CE Primary School

A Little Star

Yellow diamonds
Swirling, twirling round and round.
Gold saxophones dancing with the world.
Warm white chocolate
Melting in my mouth.
A soft, silk, yellow star
Flying in the moonlight.

Olivia Brown (9)
Burgh-Le-Marsh CE Primary School

Star Poem

Oh
Sparkling
Star burning
Bright,
Shining shadow
Light,
The glimmer point in the night.
The glittering twinkle lasting all through
The night.

Alex Holmes (9)
Burgh-Le-Marsh CE Primary School

A Golden Note

It
Is
Music
Flowing
Through my
Mind,
A saxophone blowing in the wind
Notes ringing in my ears,
The sound of music is playing,
Music going through my head.

Victoria Allen   (9)
Burgh-Le-Marsh CE Primary School

Mum

You're home-baked pizza from the warmth of sunlight,
You're the sweet delicious taste of the yellow melted cheese.
You're the happiness of God Himself,
Dancing and twirling around the clouds.
You're the warm, hot, roasting fire warming the living room,
You're the shining blue colour from the rainbow
After the wet rain which drizzles down my shoulder.
You're the blue star on a dark sparkly night,
Shining brighter than all the others.

Suzanna Hanson (9)
Burgh-Le-Marsh CE Primary School

Star

It is music
In my head, a
Saxophone blowing
In the wind.
Notes ringing in my ears, the sound of music
Is playing.
Music going through my mind, it's
Flowing through my head.

James Spence (10)
Burgh-Le-Marsh CE Primary School

Alfie

You're a brand new song,
Rocking the world,
You're a skater,
Learning to skate.

You're Cola
Dripping down my throat,
You're jeans and T-shirt
Wrapping round my body.

You're a blue river
Running through my life,
You're an egg
Slipping on my plate,
You're happiness
Improving my life.

You're shandy
In a freezing cold fridge,
You're baggy clothes,
Falling off my body.

You're a punk rock band
Rocking the world,
You're a surfer,
Learning to surf.

You're green grass
Helping me to live,
You're pasta
Wrapping round my fork.

Chad Birch (9)
Burgh-Le-Marsh CE Primary School

Star

The star soars beautifully past Earth,
Waiting around, shining in the sky,
You're a golden, shimmering object,
You're a fiery, shining fantastic
Thing.

Callum Revill (9)
Burgh-Le-Marsh CE Primary School

Star

It is music flowing through my mind.
A saxophone blowing in the wind
Notes ringing in my ears.
The sound of music is playing.
Music going through my mind.

James Paul (9)
Burgh-Le-Marsh CE Primary School

A Golden Star

You
Are a ball
Of fire, listening
To the twinkling
Tunes, flowing through
Space.
Your diamond points catch in the moonlight, lighting up
Our world, ready to explode in the night sky.

Kaylee Chadwick (10)
Burgh-Le-Marsh CE Primary School

A Normal Day

I woke up in the morning all excited and happy,
But my brother woke up miserable and snappy.
My mother asked me to go to the shop
And I ended up buying ten litres of pop.
For dinner we had sausage and chips
For dessert we had apple pips.
Next, time for the video game,
While my sister watched a horse's mane.
My brother asked me, 'Come out and play,'
'No, I'm on my video game,' I say.
Time for tea, mash, peas and meat
But I thought *pizza you can't beat,*
Then I tucked into a chocolate bar
Went outside, it flew onto a car,
Then Mum said, 'Time for bed,'
Then I said,
'No, I'm playing with my Knex benders.'
I could hear next door watching EastEnders,
Then I fell into a heap,
Nighty-night, time to sleep.

Zane Heath (10)
Burgh-Le-Marsh CE Primary School

A Midsummer Night's Dream

I will be near,
I will follow,
I will hear
Your lonely sorrow.
I will see
Your cold salty tear
I am your nightmare
From Hell.
I will tear
Your heavy heart
I will pierce it
With a blood stained dart.
I will follow you
I will play my scheme
You'll remember this time
As a midsummer night's dream.

Devon Kirk (10)
Gipsey Bridge Primary School

Devil Of The Storm

I am that magical devil of the storm
I have sharp ears and a pointed horn
I'll whiz you up and take you away
You'll never come back till break of day
I am that lightning shining bright
Waking you up and giving you a fright
I stamp my feet and clap my hands
I never listen to anyone's demands.

Holly Morgan (10)
Gipsey Bridge Primary School

I Am That

I am that mysterious sea critter of the ocean going stream
I am that wondrous creature that is a mind-blowing gleam.
I am that mischievous sprite,
Who suddenly disappears out of sight.
I am that sand monster beneath your feet,
So be careful where you put your seat.
Every step that you take
I will be there to make you shake.

Jack Jee (10)
Gipsey Bridge Primary School

You'll Never Get Away From Me

Through bush, through briar,
I'll never tire,
You'll never get away
From me!

Every cagey footstep you take
I'll be following in your wake
Every corner that you turn,
I will make your stomach churn
You never know where I could be
I could be hiding up a tree.

Through bush, through briar
I'll never tire
You'll never get away
From me.

Adam Fountain (11)
Gipsey Bridge Primary School

Anything And Anywhere

I am that merry wanderer of the night,
That lurks among the forest trees.
I am that spiky pine cone, which always seems to show,
I'm anything you think of and anywhere you go.

I am that lonely traveller
Who cries as midnight strikes.
I am a mighty gust of wind which swirls the leaves
Around your feet.
I'm anything you think of and anywhere you go.

I see your every action, I hear your every sound
I follow you here and there, I'm with you now,
So just *beware!*

Clare-Louise Twells (10)
Gipsey Bridge Primary School

Puck

Pictures can't describeth me,
For I am that merry wanderer of the night,
My fairy friends allege, 'You're a knavish little sprite,'
I lurk in a corner or up a tree but nobody,
Not even you, can find me . . .

Joshua Stones (10)
Gipsey Bridge Primary School

Woodland Spirit

I am a naughty knavish sprite
I vanish so I'm not in sight.
I'm always hidden in the light,
I am mostly made with might.

I am that lonely lover of the land,
You'll only see me on the sand.
I'll spin you round upon my hand,
So be careful where you stand.

I am that eager explorer of the Earth,
I've watched you ever since your birth.
You'll never know what I am worth,
But I'll always fill your life with mirth.

Emelia Jonsen (10)
Gipsey Bridge Primary School

A Midsummer Night Dream

A leprechaun, a knavish sprite, a master of trickery.

M adly scared to the bone, I'll be watching you day and night.
I am that jumping imp of the valley.
D on't be fooled by my shape-shifting experience
S illy me, also daft
U p and down, all around
M agically I shoot about
M usic always makes me boogie
E yes a sparkling blue, glinting in the sunlight
R ed lips like a scarlet rose.

N early dark, you get scared
I pop out of everywhere
G etting spooked I should think
H earing noises through the night
T hen you scream home to your mum.

D evilish tricks I'll play on you
R ight through the night
E ager little wicked imp
A lways playing tricks
M emory is my game I'll always remember your name!

Kate Amy Loveday (10)
Gipsey Bridge Primary School

I'll Be Watching You

I'll be watching you,
Always . . .

I'll follow you everywhere you go,
You get away from me?
Never will you escape,
Because I never tire!

I'll be watching you,
Always . . .

Every twist and turn,
I'll stalk you,
I'll turn into a tree,
How about a bush too!

I'll be watching you,
Always . . .

I'll be watching you,
Every day,
Every night,
I follow you . . .

I'll be watching you,
Always . . .

I follow you,
Into the future,
Back through the past,
I'll be watching everywhere . . .

I'll be watching you,
Everywhere . . .
Every day . . .
Always . . .

Jacob Rear (10)
Gipsey Bridge Primary School

I Am Puck

(Inspired by 'A Midsummer Night's Dream' by William Shakespeare)

I am that lonely child of the night.
I am that small and knavish sprite.
I will be a crane and make the brick drop.
It will land on your head and your life will stop.
I will always be following you.
Even if you don't want me to.
I shall be a tree and hold you tight.
You won't escape with all your might.
I will turn into mud and make a hole.
So I can trap your entire soul.
Wherever you go, whatever you do,
I will be following you.
Even if you're jumping over a log,
I will be there in the fog.
I will shape-shift into a vase with a flower,
And give a shout with my magical power.
I have two horns and am quite small,
And I'm always there when there's a call.
I shall turn into the king's crown,
And will be itchy to make him frown.
All the fairies call me Puck
And I do not bring good luck.

Paul Edwards (9)
Gipsey Bridge Primary School

Merry Wanderer Of The Night

I am that merry wanderer of the night,
I will follow you wherever you go
Through bushes,
Through trees.
I will follow you
And form a trick
I will jump and shout boo.
I am that knavish sprite,
I am that merry wanderer of the night.

Olivia Kirk (9)
Gipsey Bridge Primary School

I Am There

Every path, every track,
Every turn, every step,
Every move, everywhere,
I'll be watching.

I'm round the corners,
Up the trees,
Among the flowers,
Under the leaves,
I am everywhere.

Eyes shining through the leaves,
Ducking, weaving through the trees,
I'm invisible, hidden, I'm not there,
You cannot see me anywhere,
But beware, for I am there.

Simeon Corke (11)
Gipsey Bridge Primary School

My Guardian Friend

I am a careful, cunning friend
That makes no book nor story end.

I cheer you up when you are down
By taking away your horrible frown.

And when you die then I do too
As I am closely bound to you.

Molly Burrows (10)
Gipsey Bridge Primary School

Puck's Following You
(Inspired by 'A Midsummer Night's Dream' by William Shakespeare)

Everywhere you go, I'll follow,
Through bush and tree, I'm like a darting shadow.
Wherever you go, whatever you say,
I'll be watching throughout the whole day.

I'm always there wherever you go,
I'll follow you through wind and snow.
Wherever you are, whatever you do,
Through bog and mist I'll be behind you.

You won't notice, you won't see,
All because I'm imaginary
Don't try to turn or you'll see
A face so *scary!*

No need to run and wear out your breath,
Because I'm behind you, till your death,
You'll never make it the whole way through,
Because I'm Puck *so, sucks to you!*

Philip Lawson (9)
Gipsey Bridge Primary School

Abandoned And Alone

I am that ugly imp of the night.
Abandoned and bullied.
I never come out in the light
People stare at me and even laugh.
You would not like to look at me,
People don't like imps,
I am that ugly imp you see.

I am that hideous sprite of the dark
Everybody hates me.
I have disgusting scars and a big red mark,
I have no friends.
I just have to face being alone in the wood,
Helpless and rejected.
I just stand still and watch you where I'm stood.

Mae Davies (10)
Gipsey Bridge Primary School

My Little Brother

My little brother
As cheeky as ever
Can't speak English
But loves to mutter

He bounces all day
On my trampoline
He bounces on his bum
Like a ping-pong ball

He goes in the tub
And has a splish-splash
All plum-tucked out
He scoots off to his bed.

Sophie Smylie   (10)
Killingholme Primary School

My Box

My box is special and I will tell you what's in it.

The sound of Red Arrows zooming through the air,
The gentle breeze of summer's wind,
The swooping of a beady-eyed eagle,
The softness of the richest silk pillow,
The flash of a sun exploding.

My box has dinosaur hinges and the box is made from bones.

Hayden Taylor (9)
Killingholme Primary School

What Is Red?

Red is warm and bright
It might give you a fright.

Red is the cherry on top of a bun
Or the strawberry glowing in the sun.

Red is a roaring fire
Like my heart's deep desire.

Red is the tip of my nose
When it's cold and it snows.

Red is a London bus
Taking tourists without a fuss.

What is red?
Red is my favourite colour.

Oliver Bates (10)
Killingholme Primary School

Life

As each day passes by
People say hello,
Visitors are shown around and helped
In any way.
As the days draw a line they will
Continue in your minds.
And for a lifetime we will know
That pleasure's all around.
As each day comes again
So does happiness and fun
And when it's time
To say goodbye, the world
Will stay alight.

Nathan Oxley (10)
Killingholme Primary School

School Is Fun!

School is fun,
School is great,
Make sure you're on time,
It's no fun being late.

You meet all your friends there,
You have a good time,
When queuing for lunch,
We stand in a line.

At going home time,
We pack things away,
Go home for a sleep,
For another school day.

Jack Coupland (9)
Killingholme Primary School

Holiday Fun On The Beach

On my holiday I had great fun
Jumping over the waves in the scorching sun
Waiting for them to build up, roll over and crash
Sometimes knocking me over and making a splash!
Dashing back in and out then when I'm done
Laying out on my towel, getting dry in the sun.

Leah Kirkby (10)
Killingholme Primary School

My Dogs

I have two dogs
I always take for walks
They sit at the garden gate,
I'm sure they think they can talk.

When I come home
They're all alone,
They wait for me to play,
'Not yet,' I say
'I've got to have my tea!'

James Stockdale (9)
Killingholme Primary School

My Special Box

(Inspired by 'Magic Box' by Kit Wright)

Inside my box there are
Smiley, beaming suns in each corner
Flowers freshly picked on the top of the lid
Skeletons' fingers for the handle.

My box is a special box

My box has inside
A baby's first word
Ducks when they are first born
Beds flying peacefully through the air.

My box is a special box

My box has inside
A baby's first smile
My memories from when I was young
Freshly picked flowers.

My box is a special box

My box has inside
The memories from my uncle David
The music that makes me feel happy
The lullaby that sends you to sleep.

My box is a special box.

Victoria Vessey (10)
Killingholme Primary School

Christmas Is Here

Christmas comes once every year,
Today Christmas is nearly here.
I can hear the rhythm of *Ho Ho Ho* in my ear
Oh yes it's that time of year.
When Christmas comes beware,
The cold winds come to mess up your hair
With icicles below your nose
But you will have to let it snow
So share the festive greetings,
With lots of family meetings.
Write your Christmas list
And clench your fists
For Christmas is here!

Amy Price (8)
Killingholme Primary School

Wonder Girl!

Bored and angry needing your friends,
Want to go out to buy the new trends,
Sad and lonely, not feeling well,
But still the best wonder girl!

Sophie Stuart (10)
Killingholme Primary School

A Long Walk

(Inspired by 'Oliver Twist' by Charles Dickens)

Oliver Twist pulling straws,
Tearing, plucking, yanking,
Worried and confused,
Shaking and shivering,
Why me?
Starving and terrified,
Trembling with fear,
Embarrassed and confused,
Frightened and alarmed,
  'Please Sir, I want more!'

Georgia Copley (9)
Humberston CE Primary School

A Long Walk

(Inspired by 'Oliver Twist' by Charles Dickens)

Oliver Twist terrified, worried,
Nervous and shaking,
Why me?
Tugging the straw frightfully,
Dripping wet,
The temptation of food,
Dreadful and famished,
Walking the terror steps,
Cold and shivering,
Alarming, silence,
Getting closer and closer!
    'Please Sir, I want more!'

Francesca Wood (9)
Humberston CE Primary School

The Long Walk

(Inspired by 'Oliver Twist' by Charles Dickens)

Oliver Twist picking straws,
Scared like jelly,
Terrified like an ant,
Walking past the boys,
Frightened as a house,
Hungry as a monkey,
Desperate for some food,
Silent as the cold,
Gloomy, dark,
Mr Bumble, greedy, fat,
    'Please Sir, I want more!'

Joshua Hargreaves (9)
Humberston CE Primary School

A Long Walk

(Inspired by 'Oliver Twist' by Charles Dickens)

Short straw, bouncing heart,
Legs like jelly, terrified.

Mouth dripping, temptation,
Belly rumbling for food.

Empty footsteps, deafening silence,
'Please Sir, I want more!'

Oliver Furneaux (9)
Humberston CE Primary School

A Long Walk
(Inspired by 'Oliver Twist' by Charles Dickens)

Oh no, why me?
Starving and scared!
What shall I do?
Miserable, worried,
Please someone help me!
Dying of temptation,
My mind whizzing,
Exhausted, desperate,
My legs like jelly,
It's chilly and damp,
My tummy's rumbling,
    'Please Sir, I want more.'

Mia-Fay Harper (9)
Humberston CE Primary School

A Long Walk

(Inspired by 'Oliver Twist' by Charles Dickens)

Why me, tiny straw?
Terrified to death,
Going to be brave,
Like a super hero
Rushing to eat.
I need to eat,
The boys are starving,
Shocked, amazed,
Spooky, wet, damp hall,
    'Please Sir, I want more!'

Oliver Seddon (9)
Humberston CE Primary School

A Long Walk
(Inspired by 'Oliver Twist' by Charles Dickens)

Oliver Twist, grabbing straws,
Picks the unlucky one,
Oliver is desperate, terrified,
Legs like jelly,
Oliver dreads the walk,
Feeling depressed, sick, embarrassed,
Trembling past the boys,
Oliver feels stupid, awful,
The hall, swollen, gloomy,
Starvation reaches Oliver Twist,
Oliver faces Mr Bumble,
    'Please Sir, I want more!'

Lucy Catlyn (9)
Humberston CE Primary School

A Long Walk

(Inspired by 'Oliver Twist' by Charles Dickens)

Oh no, short straw,
Poor, petrified, lonely me
Tempted, desperate me
Wiggly wobbly legs
Old hall, chilly, small,
Almost at the cook,
　　'Please Sir, I want more!'

Joshua Blissett (9)
Humberston CE Primary School

A Long Walk

(Inspired by 'Oliver Twist' by Charles Dickens)

Hands shaking, short straw,
Piercing my heart,
Watery eyes, wobbly legs,
Trembling like jelly,
Marching like a soldier
Frozen like ice
Dark, gloomy misty hall
Tired and worn,
    'Please Sir, I want more!'

Trumann Capes (9)
Humberston CE Primary School

A Long Walk

(Inspired by 'Oliver Twist' by Charles Dickens)

No! The short straw.
Oh no, why me?
What shall I do?
Legs like jelly, help
Springs off his seat,
    'Please Sir, I want more!'

Amber Bacon (9)
Humberston CE Primary School

A Long Walk
(Inspired by 'Oliver Twist' by Charles Dickens)

Oliver Twist plucking straws,
Legs like jelly,
Sprang off his seat
Trembled gloomily down the
Gigantic long hall.
Famished with hunger.
　　'Please Sir, I want more!'

Joseph Baker (9)
Humberston CE Primary School

A Long Walk
(Inspired by 'Oliver Twist' by Charles Dickens)

Short straw pulled, alarmed,
Worried, scared, shaking like jelly,
Sprang off his seat,
Walking with terror,
    'Please Sir, I want more!'

Jack Ranson (9)
Humberston CE Primary School

A Long Walk

(Inspired by 'Oliver Twist' by Charles Dickens)

Oliver, worried and trembling,
The long walk approaching,
Embarrassed, nervous and alarmed,
Legs like quaking jelly,
Sprang off his seat,
Starved to death,
Ravenous for more,
Disobedient but affectionate,
Pestered by the boys.
    'Please Sir, I want more!'

Liam Pettinger (9)
Humberston CE Primary School

A Long Walk

(Inspired by 'Oliver Twist' by Charles Dickens)

Plucking straws, big, short,
Eager to get food.
Legs like wobbly jelly,
Face like thunder,
Alarmed by the walk,
Giddy, he walks tense,
Drifting into temptation,
Standing and scared,
'What shall I do?
Request for food,
    'Please Sir, I want more!'

Sam Lord (9)
Humberston CE Primary School

A Long Walk!

(Inspired by 'Oliver Twist' by Charles Dickens)

Oliver Twist plucking a straw,
Legs wobbling with fear,
Butterflies in his stomach,
Worried, shocked, alarmed,
Sprang off his seat,
Sweating with fear.

Niamh Tuplin (9)
Humberston CE Primary School

A Long Walk

(Inspired by 'Oliver Twist' by Charles Dickens)

Oliver Twist terrified, nervous,
'I hate long straws,'
Started to get up,
Legs like jelly,
Timid, afraid, shocked, alarmed,
Passed friends, embarrassed, trembling,
Starving in need,
In a gloomy place,
Dead silence, cold boys . . .
    'Please Sir, can I have more?'

Emily Cook (9)
Humberston CE Primary School

A Long Walk
(Inspired by 'Oliver Twist' by Charles Dickens)

Oliver Twist plucking straws,
Oh no!

Miserable, headache,
Painful feet.

Boys bellowing, tummy rumbling,
Weak, fuzzy head, exhausted.

Chilly, plain, dark and damp,
Freezing cold like ice.

Legs trembling, shaking,
    'Please Sir, I want more!'

Emily Stevenson (9)
Humberston CE Primary School

A Long Walk

(Inspired by 'Oliver Twist' 'by Charles Dickens)

Shaking like mad legs
Like jelly, sick, hungry,
Starving, alarmed, nervous, tempted,
Empty, unlucky, dead helpless,
Doomed, terrified, silent, scared,
   'Please Sir, I want some more!'

Brad Gooseman (9)
Humberston CE Primary School

A Long Walk

(Inspired by 'Oliver Twist' by Charles Dickens)

Oliver Twist sweating,
Moist, damp, dry,
Huge hall,
Got off his seat,
Legs wobbling, trembling,
Like jelly!
The straw is sharp,
Thin and shaking,
Walking, sweating,
Dangling down like a thread.
'Please Sir I want more!'

Charlie-Jade Cowling (9)
Humberston CE Primary School

A Long Walk

(Inspired by 'Oliver Twist' by Charles Dickens)

Oliver nervous and worried,
The long walk appearing,
In front of him.
Terrified and gobsmacked,
Sprang off his chair,
Tempted and ravenous,
Legs vibrating like jelly,
Pestered by the boys,
    'Please Sir, I want more!'

Henry Tasker (9)
Humberston CE Primary School

A Long Walk

(Inspired by 'Oliver Twist' by Charles Dickens)

Pulled a straw,
Leapt off my seat,
Legs like jelly,
Shaking with fear,
Oh no, why me?
Famished, ravenous,
Water dripping, marvellous food,
Belly rumbling,
'Please Sir, I want more!'

Mollie Horton (9)
Humberston CE Primary School

A Long Walk

(Inspired by 'Oliver Twist' by Charles Dickens)

Oliver tugged the straws,
Astonished, shocked, why me?
Legs like jelly,
Famished, ravenous, starving,
This is so embarrassing,
Chilly, cold, so scared,
  'Please Sir, I want more!'

Joe O'Hagan (9)
Humberston CE Primary School

The Long Walk
(Inspired by 'Oliver Twist' by Charles Dickens)

Decision made!
Hungry, rib-showing boys
Clutching empty wooden bowls
With a ferocious appetite
Having eaten every last crumb,
A dark, cold, stone hall,
With cold-blooded tables
He approached the copper
And he said,
    'Please Sir, I want some more!'

Jordan Graves (9)
Humberston CE Primary School

The Journey

(Inspired by 'Oliver Twist' by Charles Dickens)

Decision made!
Louse-like boys gathered,
Ragged, dirty boys,
Boys that have been
Starved for months.

A boy secretly knocked,
Oliver got up,
Started walking towards,
The cook,
He looked around,
And he just saw
A spider crawling through
A crack in the
Big, cold, stone hall.

Oliver was thinking he
Would get chucked out,
Into the freezing,
Streets
And never eat again,
Eventually he got to the cook.
Very nervously and slowly,
Oliver said,
    'Please Sir, can I have some more?'

Joshua Winchester (10)
Humberston CE Primary School

The Long Walk

(Inspired by 'Oliver Twist' by Charles Dickens)

Decision made,
Louse-like boys gathered,
Ragged, dirty boys,
The boys sat patiently,
Waiting for Oliver to
Ask cold, dirty boys
For more.

The cold bare rooms
The big square table,
The rotten wooden seats,
The echoey dark hall,
The gloomy dark hall.

Oliver felt nervous,
He felt scared,
But he had to
Do it.
    'Please Sir, I want some more.'

Louis Townell (10)
Humberston CE Primary School

The Trek

(Inspired by 'Oliver Twist' by Charles Dickens)

Decision made!
Louse-like boys gathered
Ragged, dirty boys,
Boneless, voracious, reckless,
Nudging and pushing,
Oliver started the journey.

Dark, gloomy, black,
Crumbled bricks,
Cracked floor tiles,
Gormless, sickly, echoey,
Bottom of the ocean,
A haunted mansion.

Scared, miserable, ragged,
Time slowly ticking,
Getting closer and closer,
Nervous, dirty, down,
Terrified as the journey goes on.

Plump, healthy, pale,
Mean, massive, ogre-like,
A hippo,
An elephant,
A monstrous creature,
The cook stood before him.
    'Please Sir, I want some more!'

Emma Brown (9)
Humberston CE Primary School

The Long Journey
(Inspired by 'Oliver Twist' by Charles Dickens)

Decision made!
Louse-like boys gathered,
Ragged, dirty boys,
Skinny, reckless, starving,
Nudging and pushing,
Oliver started trembling,
Ready for the journey.

The monstrous, gloomy hall
Echoed as Oliver walked,
Crumbling, dark and damp.

Oliver scared stiff,
Slowly looked round,
Boys winking,
Upset, reckless, miserable.

The cook stood before him,
In a dark hypnotic trance,
A big plump hippo,
Bully, overweight.
    'Please Sir, I want some more!'

Ella Goldsmith   (10)
Humberston CE Primary School

The Journey
(Inspired by 'Oliver Twist' by Charles Dickens)

Decision made,
Helpless boys gather round,
Scruffy, filthy boys,
No manners, so hungry.

Empty stone hall,
Silent, echoey dining room,
Sooty, smoky place,
Feels alive.

Petrified, scared, freezing,
Nervous, unsure,
Ragged, miserable, down,
Worried, upset.

Bully, scary, tall,
Ferocious,
As fierce as a lion,
As big as an elephant.
    'Please Sir, can I have some more?'

Sophie Goldsmith (10)
Humberston CE Primary School

The Journey

(Inspired by 'Oliver Twist' by Charles Dickens)

The decision was made!
The ragged,
Boys all gathered,
In the great stone hall.
Waiting,
Not just for food,
Oliver twist to make his move.
The hall was dark,
Damp and cold and
Like a prison.
Oliver's friend nudged him.
Oliver looked at the chef
And thought,
What a lousy, fat,
Overgrown, proud,
Elephant's bottom.
Then
    'Please Sir, I want some more!'

Jake Curtis (10)
Humberston CE Primary School

The Journey
(Inspired by 'Oliver Twist' by Charles Dickens)

Decision made!
As the boys watch in despair,
As Oliver nervously strolls
Towards the copper where
The horrid cook slowly churns
The gruel.

Oliver slowly creeps across
The creaky floor,
The cook slowly turns
His head and mumbles . . .
'What?'
    'Please Sir, can I have some more?'

Daniel Pattison (10)
Humberston CE Primary School

Oliver Twist The Journey

(Inspired by 'Oliver Twist' by Charles Dickens)

Brave decision made!
Gasping heard all around,
Silence, suddenly surrounded Oliver,
'Ask for more!'
Echoing hall repeating whispers,
Dull and dark,
'Ask for more!'
Oliver cold as ice,
Fragile feet slowly walking
Towards the big pot,
'Ask for more!'
Cook larger than Australia,
Big meanie,
Starving the children,
    'Please Sir, I want some more!'

Layla Albery (9)
Humberston CE Primary School

The Long Walk
(Inspired by 'Oliver Twist' by Charles Dickens)

Decision made!
Louse-like boys gathered,
They were ragged, dirty boys.
They nudged each other,
And drew straws.
Oliver got the shortest.
He went on the journey,
Through the cracked walls,
Nearer to the copper,
Towards the fat cook,
Massive old hall,
He was as scared as
A cat chasing a mouse.
He was nervous,
Scared, terrified, upset, voracious.
    'Please Sir, may I have some more?'

Alisha Woulfe-Flanagan (9)
Humberston CE Primary School

Harvest

H arvest is fun, it makes me cheerful
A nd it gives fruit to people
R eally harvest is great
V egetables are good for you, and you can get them at harvest
E ating vegetable is yummy
S o you can have vegetables at harvest
T o get vegetables and fruit, wait until harvest.

Sophie Pattison (8)
Humberston CE Primary School

Harvest

H appy times
A utumn days
R ipe fruit
V egetables
E njoy the celebration
S ongs for harvest
T ime to remember God.

Jack Tutass (7)
Humberston CE Primary School

Harvest

H appy to have harvest
A utumn celebrations
R ipe bananas
V egetables are shared
E njoy harvest
S haring your food
T hings to enjoy.

Rosie Pettinger (7)
Humberston CE Primary School

Fun!

Fun is multicoloured like the sparkling rainbow,
It smells like luscious lavender,
It feels like running about,
It sounds like laughter,
It looks like spring has begun,
It reminds me of being happy,
It tastes like melted chocolate dripping into my mouth!

Rawan Jaibaji (8)
Humberston CE Primary School

Fun

Fun is light green like the grass,
It tastes like wobbly jelly,
It reminds me of the ring of the church bell,
It smells like the clear fresh air,
It feels like running around,
It looks like a bunch of kids enjoying themselves,
It sounds like people screaming.

Katherine Brown (8)
Humberston CE Primary School

Fun

Fun is green like fields of clover.
Fun sounds like laughter from afar.
It always reminds me of joy and cheering.
It feels like running about and having fun forever.
It tastes like sour sweets.
It looks like the most joyful time to ever have.
It smells like freshly grown flowers from the garden.

Lani Frith (8)
Humberston CE Primary School

Happiness

Happiness is green like the shiny grass.
Happiness sounds like the birds singing.
Happiness reminds me of me getting my guinea pigs.
Happiness smells of sweet cherries just picked off a tree.
Happiness feels like sinking into a soft pillow.
Happiness looks like someone recovering from an injury.
Happiness tastes like Galaxy chocolate melting in your mouth.

Lewis Atkin (8)
Humberston CE Primary School

Greed

Greed is green like luscious grass
It smells like horrible jacket potato
It reminds me of Belgium chocolate
It sounds like the lovely kettle boiling
It looks like the digestive biscuits
It feels like the fatness
It tastes like hunger.

Dylan Thomas (8)
Humberston CE Primary School

Happiness

Happiness is yellow like a smile on your face.
It looks like my small, cuddly teddy.
It feels like a cute puppy on my lap.
It sounds like birds whistling in the air.
It reminds me of a sweet lavender plant.
It tastes of sweet Galaxy chocolate
And it smells like a scented candle
That's what I think happiness is.

Dilasha Gurung (8)
Humberston CE Primary School

Hate

The is red like a burning devil . . .
It reminds me of a really scary film . . .
It sounds like a huge gorilla . . .
It tastes like a dry Sunday dinner . . .
It looks like a plain black cat . . .
It feels like a big lump of slushy mud . . .

Alex Booker (9)
Humberston CE Primary School

Sadness

Sadness is grey like the misty smoke.
Sadness feels like a damp day.
Sadness sounds like a whale speaking.
Sadness reminds me of all the bad things in the world.
Sadness tastes like a hot feeling running down your neck.
Sadness smells like rotting bark falling off a tree.

Charlie Spencer (8)
Humberston CE Primary School

Fear

Fear is red like hot fire
It smells of smoke
It tastes of fire
It feels like a devil's horn
It looks like a devil
It reminds me of a ghost.

Alexandra Badger-Young (9)
Humberston CE Primary School

Darkness

Darkness is as black as horror.
It feels like you're going to die in painful death.
It's so, so scary, it tastes of onion.
It smells of fire burning.
It feels like you're on your own forever.
It feels like you're the only one left in your family.

Abigail James (8)
Humberston CE Primary School

Love

Love is red like a flaming red-hot love heart
Love is like a lovely, hot, gorgeous, chocolate cake
It feels like lightness through the air
It sounds like a red bumping love heart
It tastes like a lovely hot Sunday dinner
It smells like the lovely salty sea.

Harry Pask (8)
Humberston CE Primary School

Hate

Hate is dark like night
It feels like it is eating away at me
It looks like a black heart
It smells like a smoky fire
It tastes like burnt toast
It sounds like nails scraping on metal
It reminds me of a black heart.

Jacob Boden (9)
Humberston CE Primary School

Love

Love is blue like a sky on a hot summer's day
It reminds me of my best friends
It smells like a cherry cake freshly baked
It tastes like a Galaxy bar sprinkled with toffee sauce
It sounds like baby birds cheeping.
It feels like opening your presents on Christmas Day.

Eden Gabbitas (8)
Humberston CE Primary School

Hunger

Hunger is brown like soggy mud.
Hunger tastes like a fat tummy rumbling.
Hunger sounds like big crunches.
Hunger reminds me of McDonald's and pizza.
Hunger smells of juicy bacon.
Hunger feels like vibrating bellies.
It looks like a cheeseburger.

Alexander Masterton (9)
Humberston CE Primary School

Anger

Anger is red like the steam of fire
It sounds like the roar of a tiger
It reminds me of screaming and shouting
It smells like a burning heart
It feels like a huge black boulder
It tastes like chilli getting hotter and hotter in my mouth
It looks like thousands of people with red boiling faces.
      That is anger!

Daniella Baker (8)
Humberston CE Primary School

Hate

Hate is the hot blazing sun, it is red.
It reminds me of a blazing fire.
It smells like trees crashing against each other.
It looks like a devil.

Ella Fearn (9)
Humberston CE Primary School

Anger

Anger is revenge like a fire demon.
It sounds like never-ending shouting.
It tastes like a twenty-year-old, mouldy Galaxy.
It looks like darkness.
It feels like all happiness has gone forever.
It reminds me of people hitting each other.

Charlie Goodhand (9)
Humberston CE Primary School

Fear

Fear is black like a dark night.
It feels like cold water dripping on your face.
It reminds me of a volcano spitting lava.
It looks like a dark, deep, black hole.
It sounds like wind blowing in my ears.
It smells like a fire burning bright.
It tastes like a sour lemon.
Fear is black like a dark night.

Patrick Curtis (8)
Humberston CE Primary School

Fun

Fun is yellow like a beautiful melon.
It sounds like lots of terrific laughter and joy.
It smells like the fresh air coming towards us.
It feels like so many different things.
It reminds me of some people sharing and being happy.
It looks like the bright, blazing sun.
It tastes like fish and chips.

Chloe Fletcher (8)
Humberston CE Primary School

Darkness

Darkness is black like a frosty night in December.
It smells like dirty air.
It feels like ghosts creeping around.
It sounds like silence.
It tastes like broccoli.
It reminds me of Hallowe'en.

Sam Hotson (9)
Humberston CE Primary School

Coal Mine

The smell of smoke and dust,
The never-seeing light,
People just got trapped in a cave,
Suffocate they might.

Never seen the shining sun,
Never seen the moon,
Trapped in this coal mine,
Hands swollen like a balloon.

Tired and bruised,
And as brittle as a stick,
Up on my back,
Coal as heavy as a brick.

Getting put through this toil,
Is hard for people to bear,
People's life in the coal mine,
Isn't very fair.

Danielle Gorrod (10)
Humberston CE Primary School

Terrorising Train!

The hard, solid train whizzes past like a cheetah,
It's a hot fireball rolling along going 70 mph!

Its shiny silver beams sparkle from the sun's light,
Smoke from the train is thick and black,
As people shovel coal, coal going front and back.

As the driver pulls the brakes the train shivers and
Squeals as it finishes its meal of coal.

The heart-stopping noises make you want to cry out loud!
As it pulls up at the station to sleep.

Jessica Cubbison (10)
Humberston CE Primary School

Flower Seller

She walked along the hurtful street,
She had blisters all over her feet.
Her hair looked like a horse's tail,
As she walked along the rusty rail.

She hobbled along the hurtful street,
She is hoping that she will meet . . .
Someone who will be willing to pay,
A fair amount of money for the flowers she is selling today.

Georgia Strong (10)
Humberston CE Primary School

Victorian Flower Seller

The flowers are rosy red and blue.
They are yellow and orange and purple too.
My basket is brown, and is cold.
What a frozen basket I have to hold.
I don't like the darkness or the hunger.
But I have to go through.
I shiver with fear and coldness.
But I don't give up, I just carry on.
The air smells of smoke and everywhere stinks.
It smells like my hair.
My clothes are rotten and smell of glue.
My flowers are dying but still look blue.

Olivia Strong (10)
Humberston CE Primary School

The Factory

The dark dismal factory sits on the end of the cold shivering street.
The factory cries in the dead of night.
The shiny glittering moon shimmers over the factory, and the moon
Hears the factor clanking, and trying to destroy little kids for a living!

The moon walks the night
But all it can see is the factory.
The moon can see all so trust him when he says the factory is no fun
place to be.

The gruesome factory gobbles up children for breakfast and then
spits them out again.
When the sun looks over the world, a dark shadow still stays over the
factory.

Night falls again.
So trust the moon when he says the factory is no fun place to be.

Connor Masterton (10)
Humberston CE Primary School

Describing A Factory

The factory is as dull as the night sky,
The machines send shivers down my spine,
All we have to do all day is punch holes
Through the buttons and pack them into boxes.

My job is to pack them into the boxes,
It's kind of like a game of pass the parcel except it's buttons,
It's a huge building for all the process of making the buttons,
Part of the process is where the buttons are actually made,
People get scalped like a skinned sheep,
The buttons go to many different shops,
They can be sewn onto things or put onto it in a different way,
People can sew or stick them onto all different props.

Mark Siddle (10)
Humberston CE Primary School

Trains

He is a smelly and disgusting train,
Smoky, fast and heavy,
A black monster,
Screaming along the tracks.

A rocket like an explosion,
Horrible, dark and crowded,
His carriages are packed,
Noisy like a bear.

Scary like a fire
He travels quickly.

Bradley Sadler (10)
Humberston CE Primary School

Trains

The big train hurtles along the track.
Spitting out smoke and soot.
The pistons roaring like a lion.
The train's whistle sounds like a banshee.
The funnel looks like it's going to burst.

Ashley Fletcher (10)
Humberston CE Primary School

Victorian Poem

Shadowy figure walking through the town,
Constantly walking round and round.
Trying to sell her beautiful flowers,
Walking round for hours and hours.

She walks along the cobbled street,
She is hoping she will meet,
A kind person who will give,
A fair amount of money to help her live.

Poor little flowers withering in the rain,
Poor little flowers will never live again.
Forget the flowers think about her,
For diseases she is a lure.

Poor little flower girl all alone,
Walking around, she has no home.
Out from her mouth comes a little groan,
Poor little flower girl all alone.

A the end of the day,
She has no pay.

Daisy Seddon (10)
Humberston CE Primary School

My Deadly Disease

Out of the house came a deadly disease,
Through wonder it crept slowly with ease.
The creepy figure walked throughout the town,
It came poisoning people from deep down.

A spooky spell,
Felt like you was in Hell.
The disease is coming . . .
. . . coming with power and force.
Magic has been lost for evermore.

Through the door,
Through the window,
Spells have been lost forever more.
Coming through the town it roared,
'I am mighty and coming with power and force.'

Out I came with a spell,
Through the door I screamed with Hell
Now I don't feel so well.

Out the window,
Out the door,
Through the crack that was concealed no more.
Silver threats,
And silver skin
I hoped the disease wouldn't win.
I ran out in the wind
Out through the crack
Out through the door.
I screamed . . .
. . . screamed with Hell.

Lyndsey Loveday (10)
Humberston CE Primary School

Victorian Poem

From the deadly depths of Hell,
Came a flying fiery spell.
Through a crack,
And through a door,
The magic is lost for evermore.

Disease came creeping,
From deep down,
Poisoning people throughout the town.

A shadowy figure falling down,
The poor things dying in the town.

So shut your windows,
Shut your doors,
Disease is coming . . .
. . . it's coming with force!

Destroyer of families,
Bringer of death,
This is disease so beware of its wrath!

Back through the crack,
And back through the door,
The magic's concealed for evermore.

It will snap them up,
And swallow them whole,
And roar, 'I am disease,'
And sink back into the pit,
And you will see its horns as black as coal.

Saskia Wilbourne-Davy (10)
Humberston CE Primary School

The Alien

The moon is as round as a ball,
The sky is as blue as my jumper,
The stars are as bright as a light bulb,
The Earth is as round as a globe,
The space rocket is as big as a giant,
I am as small as an ant.

Jackson Woods (7)
Lisle Marsden CE Primary School

The Space Person

The stars are as white as the moon.
The moon is as bright as a bird.
The sky is as blue as the sea.
The stars are as white as a rocket.
The space rocket is as white as a seagull.
The Earth is as tiny as a dot in space.
I am excited to be going to space in a rocket.

Joshua Parrish (7)
Lisle Marsden CE Primary School

The Space Person

The moon is as white as the clouds,
The sky is as blue as a school jumper,
The stars are as glittery as a candle,
The space rocket is as big as a pyramid,
The Earth is as round as a button,
I am as happy as can be.

Lauren Stafford (7)
Lisle Marsden CE Primary School

The Space Person

The sky is as blue as the ocean,
The stars are as white as a rubber,
The space rocket is as fast as a plane,
The Earth is as round as a ball,
I am as green as grass,
I am an alien!

Olivia Probert (7)
Lisle Marsden CE Primary School

The Alien

The moon is as white as a cloud
The sky is as bright as the sun
The stars twinkle like glitter
The space rocket is as fast as a train
The Earth is as round as a ball
I am as happy as can be.

Kayleigh Wild (7)
Lisle Marsden CE Primary School

Space

The moon is as bright as a light,
The alien is as slimy as a snail,
The sun is as bright as gold,
The sky is as blue as the blinds.

The rocket is as fast as a shooting star,
The Earth is as big as a boulder,
The stars are as shiny as candlelight,
I am as excited as possible.

Mars is as red as fire,
Pluto is as blue as the sea,
Saturn is as green as grass,
Jupiter is as brown as mud,
The rocket is as spiky as a hedgehog.

Ben Fuller (7)
Lisle Marsden CE Primary School

The Alien

The moon is as white as my top,
The sky is as grey as a rain cloud,
The stars are as bright as a light,
The space rocket is as pointy as a pyramid,
The Earth is as round as a ball,
I am the same size as the alien.

David Radford (7)
Lisle Marsden CE Primary School

The Space Person

The moon is as round as a clock,
The sky is as bright as the sun,
The stars are as small as an ant,
The space rocket is as big as the school,
The Earth is as bright as the sun,
I am as green as a cabbage,
I am an alien.

William Seed (8)
Lisle Marsden CE Primary School

The Earth

The moon is as round as the Earth,
The sky is as blue as the sea,
The stars are as pointy as a pencil,
The space rocket is as tall as a giant,
The Earth is as green as grass
And as blue as the sky.

Lou Trigg (7)
Lisle Marsden CE Primary School

The Space Alien

The moon is as white as a flower,
The sky is as bright as a light bulb,
The stars are as bright as the sun,
The space rocket is as big as a skyscraper,
The Earth is as round as a button,
I am as small as a ant.

Alex Dunham (7)
Lisle Marsden CE Primary School

In Space

The moon is as round as a ball,
The sky is as blue as the sea,
The stars are as bright as the sun,
The space rocket is as fast as a cheetah,
The Earth is as small as an ant,
I am as light as a feather on the moon.

Megan Hawes (7)
Lisle Marsden CE Primary School

The Space Person

The moon is as round as a cherry,
The sky is as grey as an elephant's skin,
The stars are as big as an orange,
The space rocket is as blue as the sea,
The Earth is as small as an apple,
I am as tiny as an ant.

Kerryn Shortland   (8)
Lisle Marsden CE Primary School

The Space Person

The moon is as round as a ball,
The sky is as bright as a sun,
The stars are as bright as the sky,
The space rocket is as big as an elephant,
The Earth is as big as a tower,
I am as little as a mouse.

Natasha Ahmed (7)
Lisle Marsden CE Primary School

Space

The moon is as round as a ball,
The sky is as blue as a tent,
The stars are as small as a mouse,
The space rocket is as long as a roller coaster,
The Earth is as big as a tower,
I am as tall as a troll.

Bradley Kirk (7)
Lisle Marsden CE Primary School

The Space Person

The moon is as bright as the sun,
The sky is as blue as the sea,
The stars are as bright as lion's eyes,
The space rocket is as pointy as a pyramid,
The Earth is as small as a car,
I am as excited as a schoolboy on his birthday.

Joseph Short (7)
Lisle Marsden CE Primary School

The Space!

The moon is as white as a piece of paper,
The sky is as blue as our jumpers,
The stars are as shiny as a torchlight,
The alien is as ugly as a gorilla,
I am as little as a cat,
The Earth is as round as an apple.

Luke Codd (7)
Lisle Marsden CE Primary School

The Space Alien

The moon is as beautiful like a cherry,
The sky is as blue as a flower,
The stars are as bright as a lion's mane,
The space rocket is as fast as a cheetah,
The Earth from space looks like a button,
I am as small as a worm.

Liam Murtagh (7)
Lisle Marsden CE Primary School

The Adventure

The moon is as white as a rubber,
The sky is as blue as my teddy,
The stars are as shiny as a light bulb,
The space rocket is as fast as a cheetah,
The Earth is as big as a giant,
The alien is scary as a T-Rex
I am small as a fly.

Loretta Hall (8)
Lisle Marsden CE Primary School

Space

The moon is as white as a piece of paper,
The sky is as blue as the wallpaper,
The stars are as golden as a ring,
The rocket is as big as a pyramid,
The Earth is as big as a giant.
I am as small as a snake.

Oliver Baxter (8)
Lisle Marsden CE Primary School

Blast-Off

Vibrating, screeching, rocking, rattling,
Rustling, roaring, cheering,
Quaking, disappearing, appearing.

Into orbit
Whirling, whizzing, floating,
Investigating, wheeling,
Glowing, crashing.

Landing
Rescuing, grounding, sizzling,
Crackling, falling, smashing,
Smoking, burning.

Jack Crichton (8)
Lisle Marsden CE Primary School

Blast-Off

Tumbling, screeching, shaking,
Screaming, cheering, swaying,
Roaring, vibrating,
Rattling, whistling.

Into orbit
Spinning, turning, travelling,
Rounding, wearing,
Turning, floating,
Investigating, looking, staring.

Landing,
Falling, crashing, smashing,
Sizzling, burning,
Smoking, splashing, rescuing,
Cheering, shouting.

Zara Dawson (8)
Lisle Marsden CE Primary School

Blast-Off

Counting down, rising,
Vibrating, cheering, loud,
Roaring, shaking, screeching,
Rumbling, quaking.

Orbit
Spinning, circling,
Asteroids, stars, planets,
Zooming, going fast,
Malfunction, repairers going home.

Landing
Screeching, clapping,
Crashing, very loud, cheering,
Slowing down, shaking,
Stopping.

Louis Wheelton (8)
Lisle Marsden CE Primary School

Blast-Off

Vibrating, screeching, cluttering,
Rattling, speeding, shaking,
Crackling, tumbling, rumbling,
Quaking, wobbling, pinging.

Into orbit
Spinning, floating, rotating,
Rounding, turning, flying,
Whirling, travelling, circling,
Rotating, pushing, crowding.

Landing
Sluggish, deafening, crashing,
Smashing, ear-splitting,
Exploding, zooming,
Smoothly, noisily, stopping.

Thomas Chessman (8)
Lisle Marsden CE Primary School

Blast-Off

Vibrating, rumbling, roaring,
Heating, crashing, crackling.

Into orbit
Shaking, quaking, circling,
Rounding, whirling, travelling.

Landing
Whirling, falling, diving,
Splashing, blooming, smashing,
Burning, smoking, sizzling.

Rebecca Burrows (8)
Lisle Marsden CE Primary School

Mars - Haiku

Mars has got rivers
Astronauts go to see it
Mars is red and black.

Jacque Barnes (8)
Lisle Marsden CE Primary School

Planet - Haiku

Venus has puddles
And it has skies of fire
A planet of rocks.

Alfie Ney (7)
Lisle Marsden CE Primary School

In Neptune - Haiku

My rocket is fast
I like the planet Neptune
Back at home at last.

Tyler Wells (8)
Lisle Marsden CE Primary School

Saturn - Haiku

The planet with rings
Saturn is a huge planet
Astronauts go there.

Jack Paddison (8)
Lisle Marsden CE Primary School

Uranus

It sits in black space,
Uranus has blue rings round it,
Space is black and has stars.

William Paddison (7)
Lisle Marsden CE Primary School

In Saturn - Haiku

I like red Saturn
I jump into the rocket
It is a gold spaceship.

Connor Neal   (8)
Lisle Marsden CE Primary School

Neptune - Haiku

There's no gravity,
I jumped very high in space,
The planet is blue.

Jaelle Walker (8)
Lisle Marsden CE Primary School

My Family

M y mum is the best
Y es that's the truth

F amily are the best of all
A nd my name is Nicholas Hawke
M atthew is a little monkey
I have a dad called Edward
L ittle Benjamin, he is cute
Y et he won't be the youngest for
    Long, another baby's coming along.

Nicholas Hawke (10)
Market Rasen CE Primary School

Rabbit

R abbit bouncing in the sun
A t the oak tree he does it most
B ouncy hop, bouncy hop
B ut always runs away from foxes
I t is fun bouncing with them
T hey do it all day long.

Rebecca Dame (9)
Market Rasen CE Primary School

I Like Animals

I like rabbits
They go hoppity hop
I like cats that lie by the fire that goes
Poppity pop
I like frogs
That feed upon flies
I like birds
That fly in the skies
I like dogs
That wag their tail
I like mice
That are sweet without fail
But the animal I like to be
Is very simple and that is me.

Frances Haley (9)
Market Rasen CE Primary School

I Like Football Because . . .

Football is the best game in the world.
Football makes me happy and fills my body with joy.
You can play football whether you are a girl or boy.
Football is my favourite game for seven days of the week
And 356 days a year.
I like it when my mum and dad come along to watch and cheer.

Football is a game full of energy and fun.
Football is played in the snow, rain and sun.
When I play football I like to score.
One goal is good but a hat-trick is more.

My knees get dirty and my kit is too.
My mum says never mind, it's into the bath with you.

George Bennett (9)
Market Rasen CE Primary School

Animal

A ntelopes look very stunning and they love running
N ewts have lots of scales and small colourful tails
I nsects aren't very sleepy but they're always creepy
M alayan tapirs like to swim but they're not very slim
A sian elephants are loud on their feet because they love to eat
L emurs are black and white and they have brilliant sight.

Amber Bowyer (9)
Market Rasen CE Primary School

Outside

The sky is grey
No clouds to see
The branches bend and sway
But what about me
I can't go out to play
Because it's going to rain on me.

Mason Dawson (9)
Market Rasen CE Primary School

Animals

A nimals are fun, some of them make me laugh
N aughty elephants squirt water at me
I n the stable where horses sleep there is a foal
M ummy horse is healthy and so is the foal
A nts love to dig and carry leaves
L eaping kangaroos, oh look a little Joey
S orry to say but that's the end of my poem.

Kate Cooling (9)
Market Rasen CE Primary School

The Four Seasons

Spring brings light, blossom and flowers
Summer brings sun and rain
Autumn brings harvest and the trees drop their leaves
Winter covers the landscape with a white blanket of snow
And that is the end of a year.

Harry Weatherall (9)
Market Rasen CE Primary School

My Dog Poppy

This is a poem about a dog called Poppy
Whose ears are really floppy
She likes to chew her toy
But really acts like a boy
Her hobby is smelling cheese
And stealing my mum's keys
She really likes my dad
But when she goes too far my dad gets mad
She also likes my mother
But mostly likes my brother
She also likes to chew the mail
And after that she wags her tail
Her favourite toy is her ball
But mostly it goes over the wall
She likes to smell the flowers
And my mum's favourite cauliflowers
When I start to giggle
She suddenly starts to wiggle
When she suddenly starts to itch
Her nose will start to twitch.

Georgia Eshelby (9)
Market Rasen CE Primary School

Hate

It looks like something really disgusting and very sad
It smells like something really disgusting and really smelly
It feels like runny chocolate pouring out of a cup
It reminds me of when my brother said he hated me.

Megan Gardner (7)
Market Rasen CE Primary School

The Dreadful Poem

It sounds like people are eating
With lots of people having a tug of war.
It feels like a really tough tug of war with ten people doing it
And they are falling over.
It tastes like an explosion in my bedroom!
It reminds me of the horrible cybermen from Doctor Who!
It looks like a dreadful hamster that is beating us all the time.
It smells like a slitheen doing what it always does.

Esther Robinson (7)
Market Rasen CE Primary School

Fear

It tastes like pink slimy worms
It looks like a big ball of sadness
It reminds me of puppies that are homeless
It smells like a pair of smelly socks
It sounds like a crash on the ground
It feels like a sharp smooth knife.

Holly Butterworth (7)
Market Rasen CE Primary School

My Pets

My gerbils are funny
They don't like honey
They like to play
They run around the cage all day
They are funny and small
They have a small ball
When they go to sleep
They roll into a ball
When they stand on their back legs
They are very tall
I used to have a hamster who was slow
He liked to stay low
He slept all day
When he was awake
We used to play.

Daniel Young (9)
Market Rasen CE Primary School

Poetry About Tyson

Tyson is a dog who is really good
When it rains he plays in the mud
Tyson is a very good boy
And Tyson loves to chew his toy
When you put your fingers up, he gives you his paw
And when he wants some tea, he always has more
When he is naughty my dad goes up the wall
But when he is good my dad throws a ball
When he comes in
My dog smells the bin
My dog is a rottweiler which means he can bite
Sometimes he chases a kite
Sometimes my dog tries to bite his leg
My dog has a toy which is called Ted.

Aaron Briggs (10)
Market Rasen CE Primary School

My Sister Tori

I'm about to tell you a story
About my sister Tori.
I love it when you squeeze me
I hope you never leave me
I love it when you sing
You are just like an angel but with a red wing
You're the best sister I could ever have
And I hate it when you are mad
I never want to see you sad
I love it when you play with me
And sometimes pay for me
At the movies
And sometimes you buy me a smoothie
I love it when you make our tea, it always tastes delicious
But it's a bit suspicious.

Emma-Jane Hordon (9)
Market Rasen CE Primary School

Happiness

What does it look like?
It looks like a sweet tasty chocolate cake.

What does it taste like?
It tastes like a hot dog with some tomato sauce
And with a hot sausage.

What does it remind you of?
It reminds me of a burger with some tomato in.

What does it sound like?
It sounds like a ladybird.

What does it feel like?
It feels like a rough mat.

Riegan Carlton (7)
Market Rasen CE Primary School

Hallowe'en

I love Hallowe'en
I like it when I get a jelly bean
There is a little rhyme that people say
I'm not going to say it, because you might go away.

I'll go treating for an hour or two,
They'll give me sweets, maybe candyfloss too.

Alice Rice (10)
Market Rasen CE Primary School

Love

It reminds me of having a beautiful time in my wonderful,
Pretty, cosy, warm house.
It feels like my enjoyable, comfy, soft and bouncy bed at night
When the stars are out, shining bright.
It tastes of a delicious cheeseburger with cheese, tomatoes and
cucumber.
It looks like fresh, cold green rich, golden grass blowing in the wind.
It sounds like my beautiful, wonderful, lovely, family watching TV.
It smells of wonderful, cooked delicious hot BBQs in the summer sun.

Kieron Paul (7)
Market Rasen CE Primary School

Fear

It smells like people's disgusting smelly breath.
It tastes like dreadful snake-like grass.
It looks like people arguing, fighting.
It reminds me of when I first met Ryan and Daniel.
It feels like punching and kicking.

Jarrad Dawson (7)
Market Rasen CE Primary School

Sadness

It looks like playing in the fields
It tastes like fresh air
It smells like blood from dead people.

Abbie Sellars (8)
Market Rasen CE Primary School

Sadness

It sounds like people whinging.
It tastes like orange juice.
It smells like green grass.
It looks like people crying.
It feels like horrible, stinky clay.

Oliver Boylan (7)
Market Rasen CE Primary School

Hate

It feels like a big fight and they're attacking each other.
It sounds like a big meteorite right next to me.
It looks like an explosion near me.
It tastes like a burnt sausage.

Alexander Hodgkinson (7)
Market Rasen CE Primary School

Prince And The Princess

I'm locked up in a tower,
All I have is this flower,
My prince should be coming, in a hour,
Until then I will stay in my tower.

I hope nobody's forgotten me,
As you see my name is Penelope
And no one should have forgotten me
Just walk by, and there's Penelope.

As you see I'm a princess,
I think I might need to confess,
For this I need Mum's red dress,
I think we might make a mess,
So don't be a little pest.

Right, here I am in Mum's red dress
And every word ends in the letter s
Right now, make a mess,
That's how to be a little pest,
And that's why Mother (the queen) hates little pests.

It's been an hour,
In my tower,
Wait a minute, is that a prince,
This may be my chance,
Wait is he glancing,
It must be at me,
'Cause I'm a fantasy, Penelope.

Laura Walott (7)
Pinchbeck East Primary School

Hallowe'en

Vampires, zombies and pixies
All walking down the streets
Scientists, mummies and witches
With bags full of sweets.

Skeletons, elves and bats
Light pumpkins in the park
Ghosts, gnomes and cats
All coming out at dark.

Aliens, werewolves and pirates
Knocking on people's doors
Trolls, dragons and wizards,
All lighting pumpkins outdoors.

Lucy Seymour (8)
Pinchbeck East Primary School

The Princess

There once was a princess who lived in a castle
She stayed in her room because it was much less hassle,
She read a book and went on an adventure,
Wondering where the book would take her,
It took her to lots of wonderful places,
And met new people, new faces,
She had so much fun not being alone,
She went back home and got on the phone,
She called up all her friends and mates,
Invited them to her castle to bake some cakes,
Because she had such a fun-filled day,
In her room she no longer wanted to stay.

Megan Edwards (8)
Pinchbeck East Primary School

My Friend Jake

I have a friend, his name is Jake
His hair is black as coal.
He saw a rabbit the other day and chased it down a hole.
His ears are really floppy and as soft as silk to touch.
Jake he is the best dog and I love him very much.

Amy Wilson (8)
Pinchbeck East Primary School

It's Harvest Time

You can beep the horn,
When you can see some corn
It's harvest time again
It's time to get your pen
Apples so, so red
And when your face is going so, so red,
You know it's harvest time again.

Layla Alexander (8)
Pinchbeck East Primary School

My Little Penny Puppy Dog

Her fur is white
Her eyes are bright
She loves to play all day
And cuddles in a ball at night
For her good behaviour she earns a treat
Which is usually meat
All the family loves our Penny, and so many more
As you would find it you came to our door.

Lucy Barley (9)
Winterton Junior School

Bob And Bill

Bob and Bill are my two fish
And they always look so sad
But when Mum and Dad go to bed
They party down like mad.

One night I came down so late
And let their friends in our gate
Scruffy cat, the itchy dog
A parrot, a budgie and even a frog.

Bob played piano, Bill sang the songs
Scruffy tooted her trumpet
Itchy clanged the gong.

Then the animal band heard
Mum and Dad stomping
Down the stairs then
They got there and . . .

Corrianne Gray (8)
Winterton Junior School

My Cat

I love my cat, he's so cool,
He sometimes follows me to school.
But when I'm home at half-past three,
He miaows loudly for his tea.

He sometimes brings my mum a mouse,
She screams when it runs round the house.
I still love him most of all,
When he curls up in my shawl.

Danielle Preskey (8)
Winterton Junior School

Rosie The Cat

I have a cat called Rosie
She is really quite dozy
Her colours are black and white
She tends to stay out for the night
When you see her eyes so bright
She loves to have a good old cuddle
And likes to play with wool in a muddle.
Her favourite food is chicken and tuna
But doesn't like lamb Tikka Bhuna.

She chases birds, hedgehogs and frogs
It would be nice to see her chase the noisy dogs!
She really would like to sleep on my bed
But she's such a fidget she'll end up on my head
She's only attracted to small children,
And won't go near my mum's cauldron.

Holly Welsh (9)
Winterton Junior School

My Cheeky Little Puppy Boo

Be careful when you come in
Or your shoes will be nicked,
Sooner or later you will find them gone,
In my dog's mouth you will find them.
If you bring your child be careful,
Or you might come back with your child upset
By fluff everywhere and toys chewed.
If we bring our puppy be careful
If you have a garden, or there will be lots of holes in your garden.
Be careful if you let your dog with ours or they'll fight,
But I like my cheeky little puppy, Boo, just the way he is.

Molly Brocklebank (8)
Winterton Junior School

A Windy Day

Today was very windy,
The wind blew off my hat,
Then my gloves, my scarf as well
And my coat went after that.

The wind blew fast, the wind blew hard.
It whistled right through my backyard!
Around my feet, the leaves did dance,
Then it blew off my underpants!

Georgia Ashton (9)
Winterton Junior School

My Family

There are three people in my family,
Mum, Dad and me.
My dad likes to play the guitar,
When my mum goes to work she travels quite far!
I have three pets, a dog, a cat and a guinea pig,
Hey! My dad's not bald and doesn't wear a wig!
Now that was a bit about my family,
I hope to see you if you come round for tea!

Sophie Thompson (9)
Winterton Junior School

Winter Wonderland

The snow falls down in the big, white sky
As Father Christmas is passing by.
Rudolph with his big red nose,
All the snowflakes start to pose.

Jack Frost is playing his game
Ploughing and throwing frost again.
Waiting to open presents under the tree
And for Santa to come to me!

Benjamin Johns (8)
Winterton Junior School

My Family

My mum is loads of fun,
She buys me pants,
To cover my bum.

My dad is very bad,
I think he's gone
Quite mad.

My sister has a blister,
On the end of her nose,
Of course she has a plaster,
But it blocks up her crows.

My brother is another,
Alien from outer space.
I guess that's not so weird,
As we're here to
Destroy the human race!

Julian Buckley (8)
Winterton Junior School

Scat The Cat

I'm Scat the cat, I'm the only one of my kind,
I run, I fight and I have a nasty bite.

I'm Scat the cat, my friend is Blue the cat, and
Let me tell you this for free,
I'll miaow and pull, I'm never merrier than when eating snacks,
Or just being me.

I'm Scat the cat, though my owner tells people am good,
So I hiss at her friends and water her plants
To make sure that's quite understood.

I'm Scat the cat, when I'm called am straight for my meal!
Then I share it with my friend called Blue.

I'm Scat the cat, when am called bad and my tail is quite still,
As for a snack, it's like a pat on the back,
I tell you I really can't fail.

I'm Scat the cat, I'm everyone's friend except from my owner's dad,
When there's a biscuit or titbits,
I really don't mind,
After all a cat has to live.

Kirsty Nundy (9)
Winterton Junior School

Months Of The Year Poem

January is the start of the year
February is next and very near
March begins the start of spring
April is dull and always raining
May is there to chase the rain away
June the sun comes out to play
July the sun is still quite bright
August is nice and even hot at night
September is boring, we go back to school
October I go trick or treating, it is really cool
November there are lots of fireworks, what a fright
December, hooray, we get lots of presents, it's a snowy night.

Natalia Dobbs (7)
Winterton Junior School

Who's The Boss?

My dad thinks he's the boss
He shouts and stomps and gets real cross.

My mum says that she's the chief
But all she does is give me grief!

My baby sis reckons she's the leader
She's only quiet when we feed her!

Even the dog thinks he's the best
Bark, bark, bark, there is no rest!

I can't wait until I've grown
I'll move out and live alone
I'll be as quiet as a mouse
And I'll be the boss in my house!

Jessica Ashton (10)
Winterton Junior School

My Dogs

My dogs are black and white
They scatter round the kitchen floor
Waiting for an open door
Scratching their paws
Wagging their tails
Barking loudly if all else fails.

Emma Reid (7)
Winterton Junior School

Ten School Computers

Ten school computers all sat in line,
One broke down, then there were nine.

Nine school computers all running late,
One exploded, then there were eight.

Eight school computers coming up from Devon,
One got lost, then there were seven.

Seven school computers all in a mix,
One walked off, then there were six.

Six school computers all alive,
One didn't work, then there were five.

Five school computers broke a law,
One went to jail, then there were four.

Four school computers hiding near a tree,
One was late, then there were three.

Three school computers all stuck with goo,
One jumped in a pond, then there were two.

Two school computers singing a song,
One lost his voice, then there was one.

One school computer sitting all alone,
No one there to talk to, so he went home.

No school computers sitting two by two,
No work for us . . . what's Mrs Vernau going to do?

Jessica Barley (8)
Winterton Junior School

Fruit And Vegetables

C runch crunch
A carrot
R eally really nice
R eady washed and peeled
O range like an orange ball
T he only difference is it does not bounce!

A round juicy ball
P erfect for you
P erfect for me
L ovely red apples
E at one for tea!

P ears on a tree
E at them hot or cold
A healthy fruit
R eady to eat

C orn on the cob
O h what a mess
R eally sweet
N ot easy to eat!

Katie Waters (7)
Winterton Junior School

In The Garden

In the garden where green grass grows,
There are flowers and trees and shrubs and hedgerows.

In the spring when daffodils show
Tulips and crocuses also do grow
There are snowdrops all white and bluebells so blue
So when you're out in the springtime look around you.

A garden in summer is colourful and bright,
The roses and climbers are such a beautiful sight.
Every colour is here, the weather's so sunny,
Bees buzz around, collecting pollen for honey.

In autumn the trees so green with their leaves
Have changed different colours and fallen from the trees.

In winter bare branches are covered in frost
The colours from summer all hidden and lost.
The snow will come, it makes such a sight,
It covers the garden in a blanket of white.

It's great to be in a garden each day
Where plants and flowers grow in every way.

Chloe Darnill (8)
Winterton Junior School

My Brothers

My brothers always make me laugh
They really are so funny,
I play games with them in the garden
When it is nice and sunny.
My eldest brother plays a guitar
And he has very long hair,
If ever I get sad or bored
I know that he'll be there.
My other brother watches wrestling,
And always plays football,
When I need help with anything
He never minds at all.

Alysha Harvey (7)
Winterton Junior School

Rapunzel, Rapunzel

'Rapunzel, Rapunzel with
Hair so fine, come out your
Window, climb down the vine.'

'The feat you ask is not so easy,
I don't respond to that line because it's
Far too cheesy.'

'Oh please, oh please come down that
Vine,
Or else I cannot give you this heart of mine.'

'Oh fine, oh fine, I'll come down the vine
But I have to be back for half-past nine.'

Laura Clixby (9)
Winterton Junior School

I've Got Jelly In My Pants Miss

(Based on 'Please Mrs Butler' by Allan Ahlberg)

'Miss he's put jelly in my pants what should I do?'
'Go into the toilet, flush it down the loo,
Do what you want girl, but don't get me into a curl.'

'Please Miss, it's not fair Miss,
It's true that boy really did put jelly in my pants Miss.'

'Stop, stop, stop, girl why would he do such a silly thing girl?
Hullabaloo, no more girl!'

'If you want some advice Miss,
I have wanted to say this all year Miss,
You belong in a zoo!'

Jack Smallcombe (9)
Winterton Junior School

My Ice Cream!

My ice cream is wonderful,
With five chocolate flakes!
Chocolate, strawberry and vanilla ice cream
And rainbow sprinkles.

A double cone,
With melted chocolate.
Strawberry and raspberry sauce!

Banana or strawberry chunks,
Which one?
I'll have both
My ice cream is such bliss!

Rebecca Cobb (10)
Winterton Junior School

The Rhino Rap

He's big and hairy
Bulgy eyes
A really big horn
He'll make you cry
Because he's my
Rhinosaurus.

Naomi Byrne (10)
Winterton Junior School

Rise Up And Shine

Rise, rise
Rise up and shine
It's time to get up time.

The church bells are ringing,
All the birds are singing
Get up, get up, get up.

The trees are swaying
Children are playing
Get up, get up, get up.

Quick, hurry, got to dash
That's it, *splash!*

Hollie Hillsdon (11)
Winterton Junior School

Sammy's Life

My name is Sammy and I'm 13 weeks old
I live with the Stricklands and I like it very much
I'm black all over, apart from my paws and my stomach
I am very playful and love to chew paper
I also love to play with my noisy toys
My favourite food is bacon and I'm very curious
I love to be fussed a lot and I purr too
I sleep in different positions and love my owner's bed
I adore my life at the Stricklands and I hope you'll enjoy this book
Because I always meet new people everywhere I look.

Gemma Strickland (9)
Winterton Junior School

A Summer's Moon And Roses

A summer's moon and roses,
Roses shine throughout the day,
And the full moon twinkles,
In April and May.

A winter's moon and starlight,
Starlight guides Santa's sleigh,
And the full moon stays out,
On the beginning of a snowy white day.

An autumn's moon and leaves,
Leaves fall silently down.
Clouds get in the way of the moon,
As the owl's hoots echoes around.

A spring's moon and blossom,
Blossom blooms on the trees,
The full moon shines,
And the birds are flying free!

Megan Mumby (7)
Winterton Junior School

Autumn

The days are short
The nights are long
Where have all the birds
And animals gone?
The plants and flowers
Start to die away
I hope to see them one more day
How I long for spring to come,
To feel and see the morning sun.

Jake Frame (9)
Winterton Junior School